FISH

ADULT COLORING BOOK
LUXURY EDITION

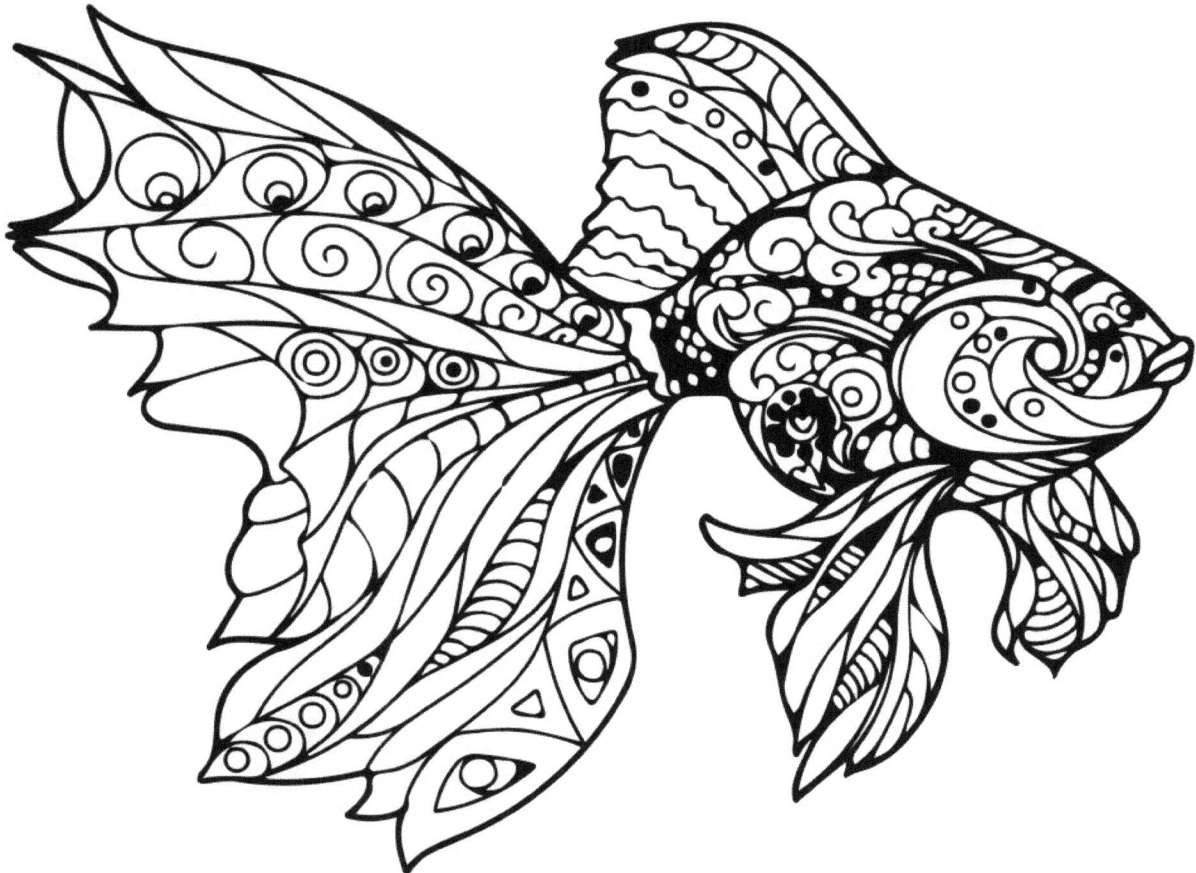

David C. Morgan

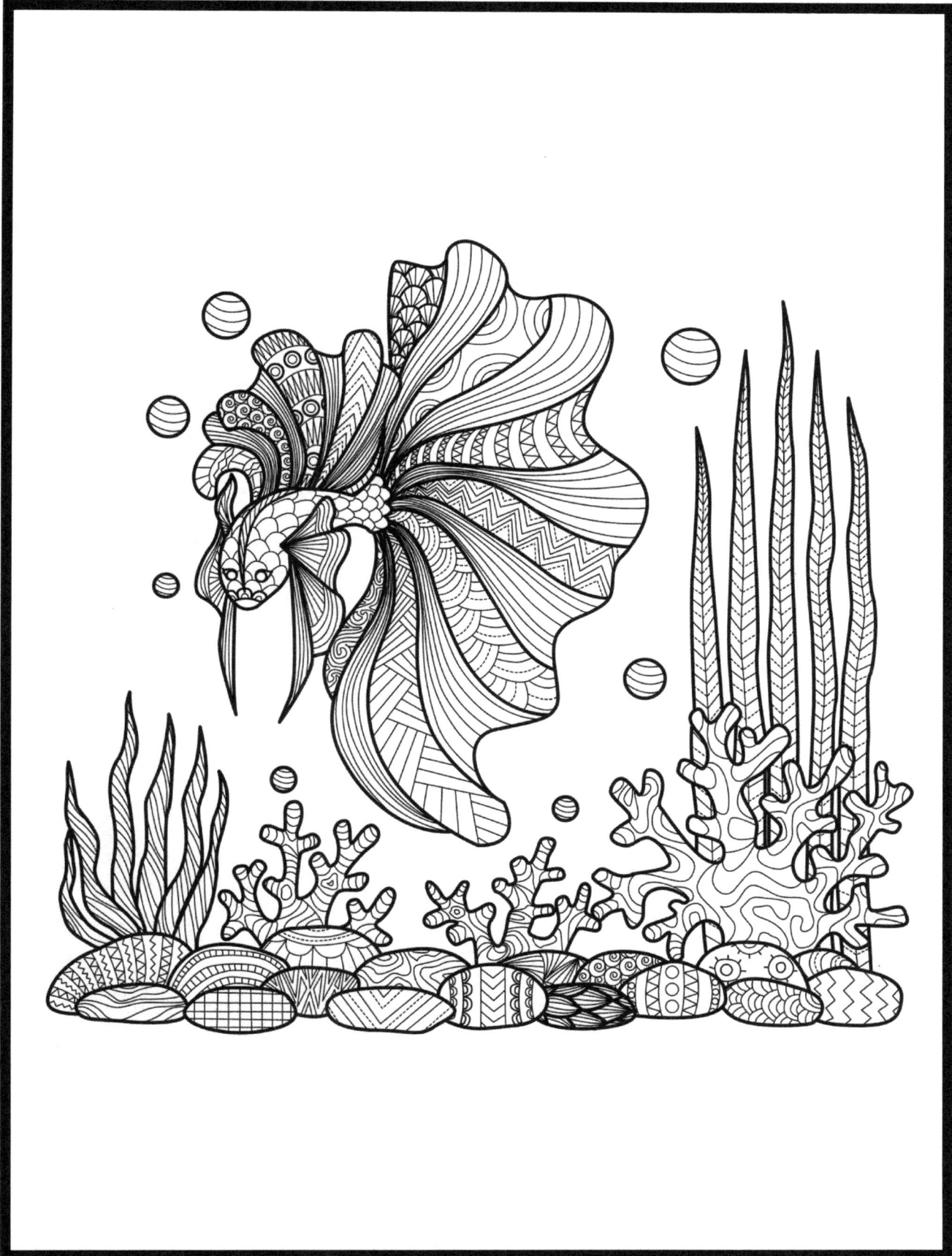

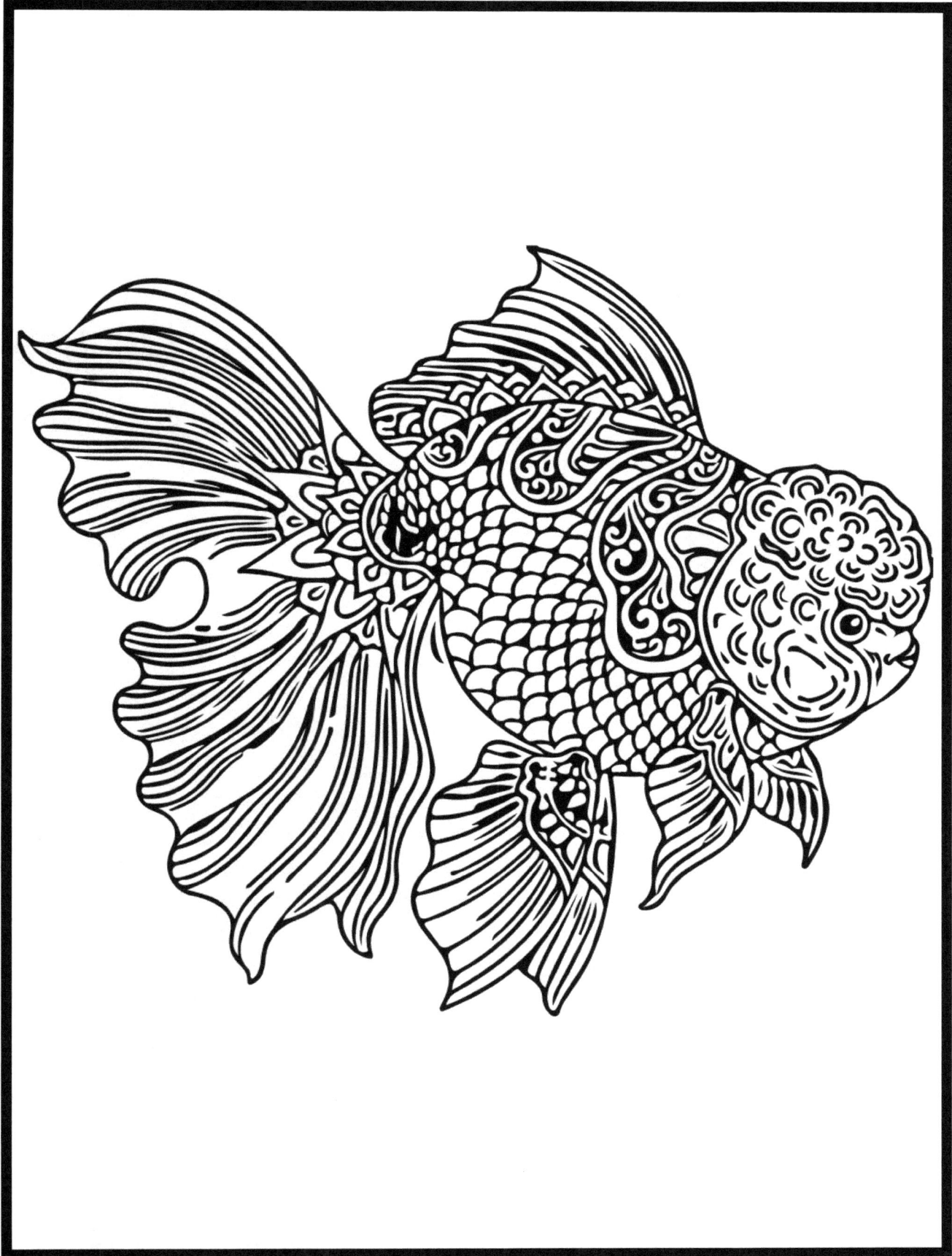

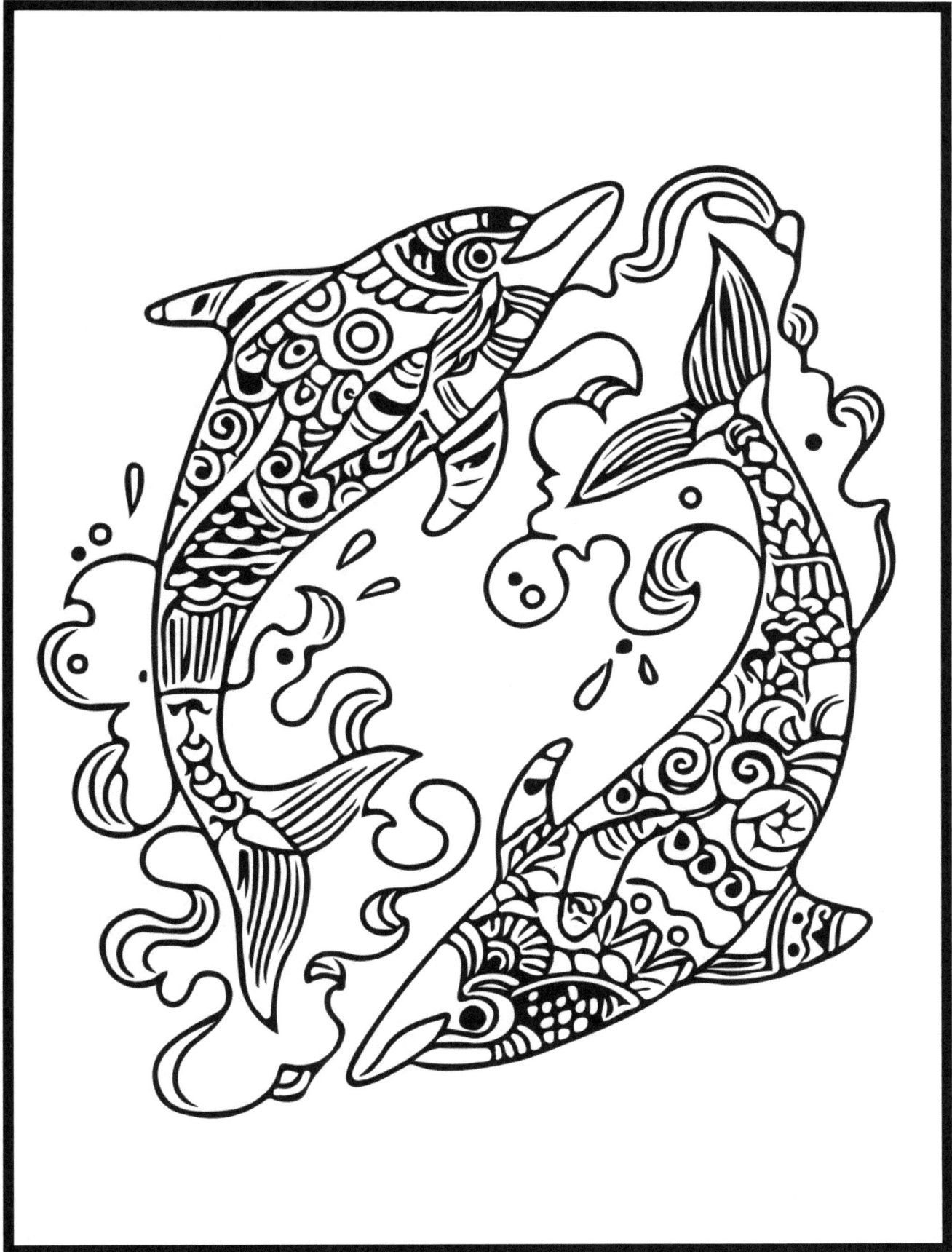

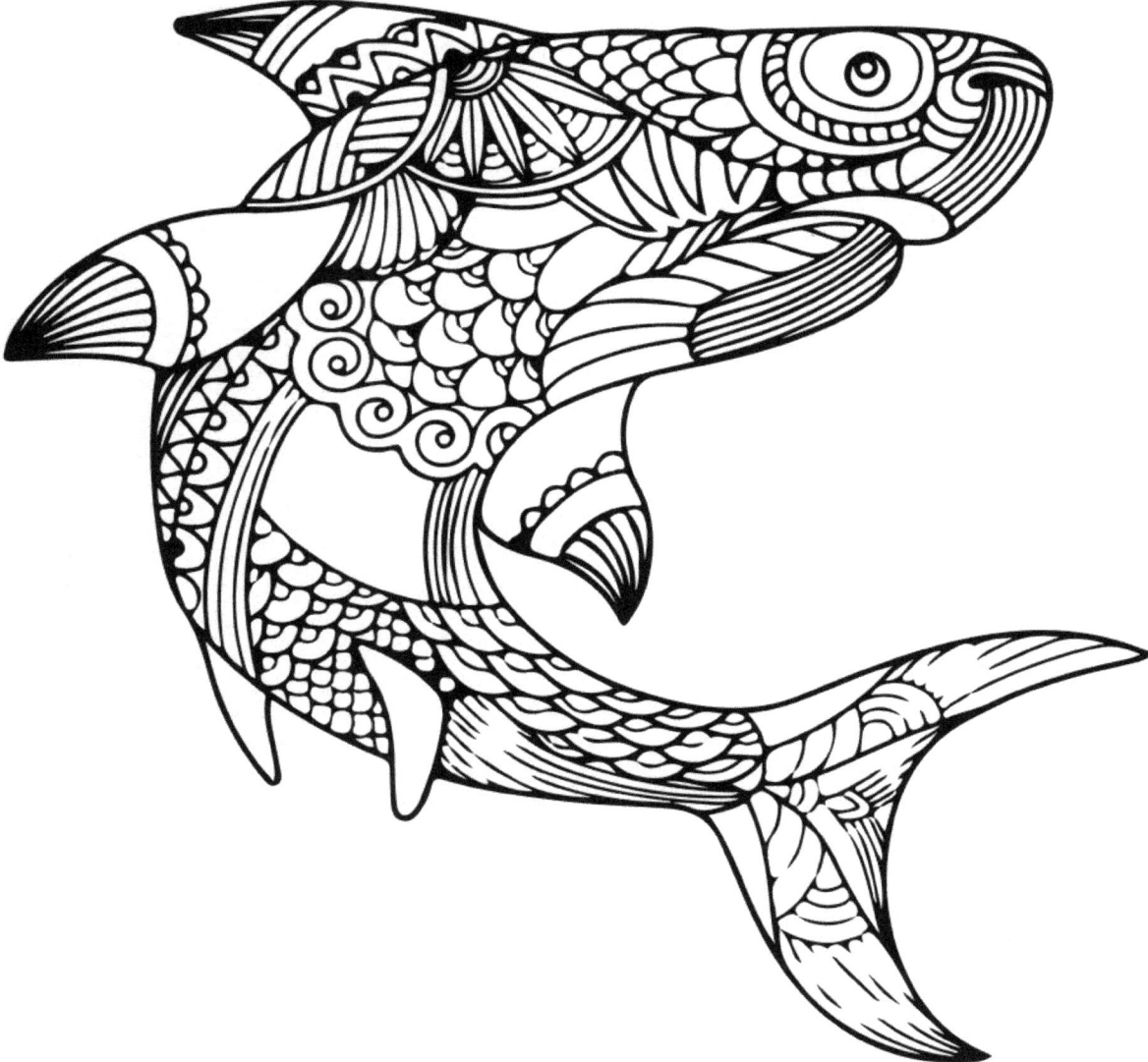

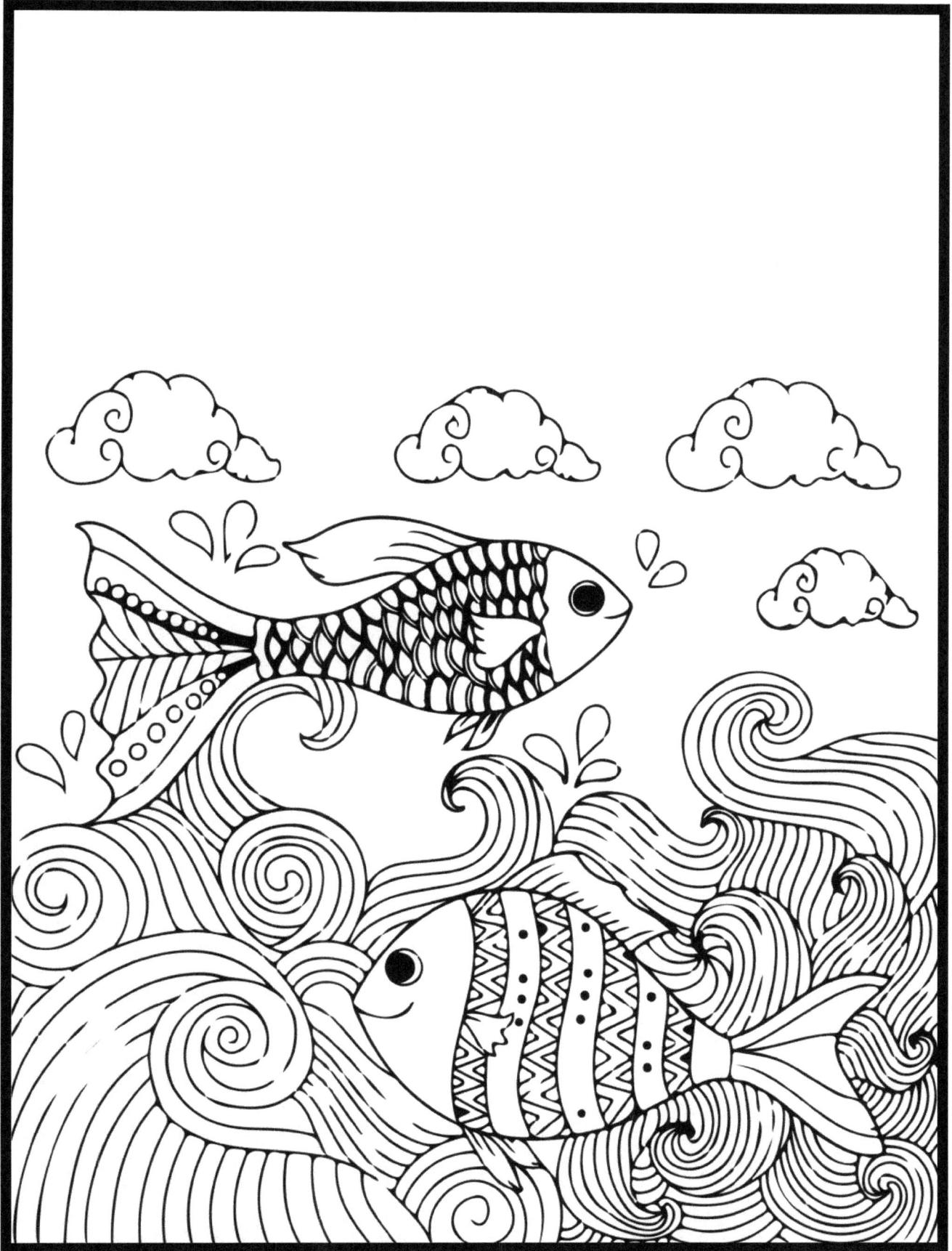

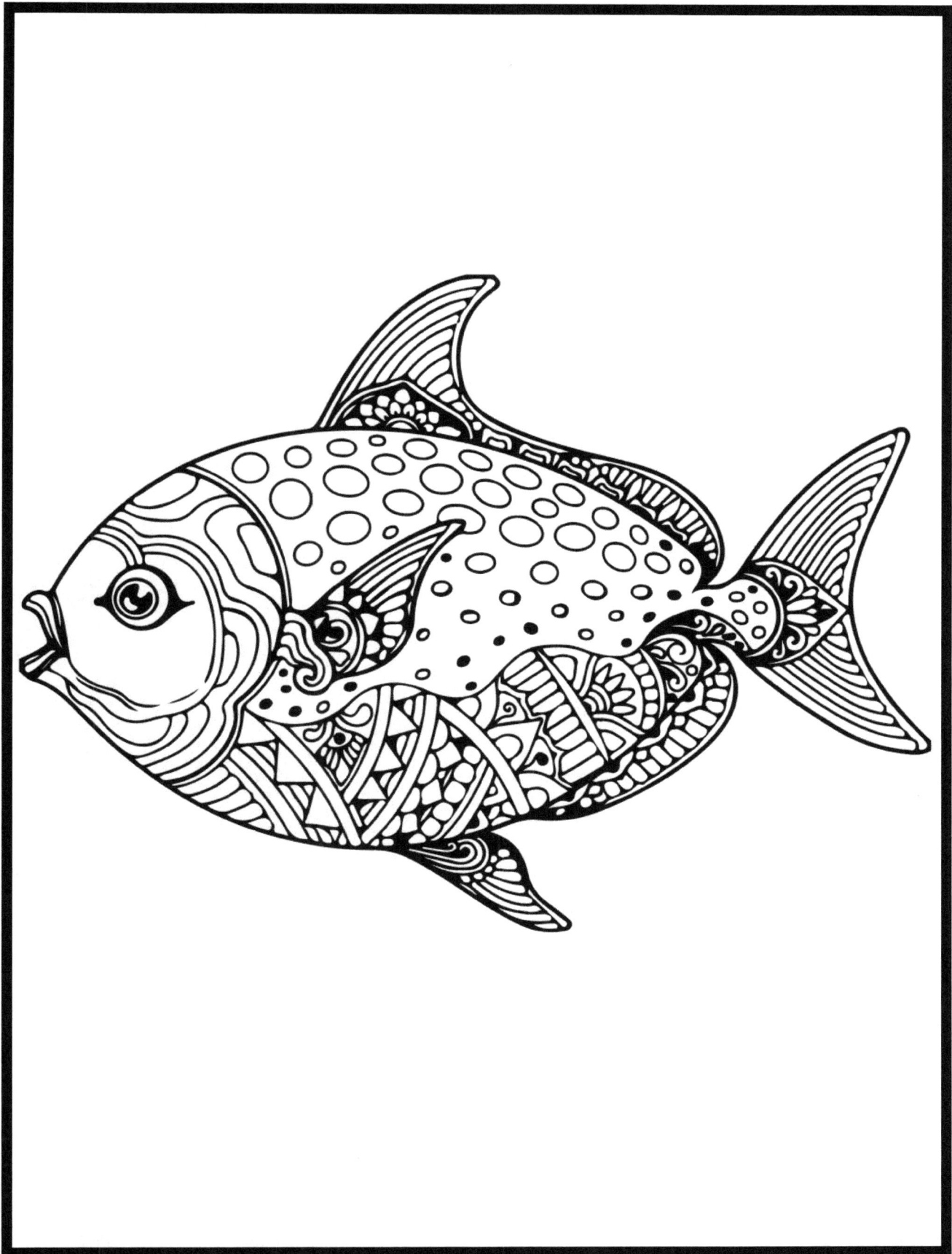

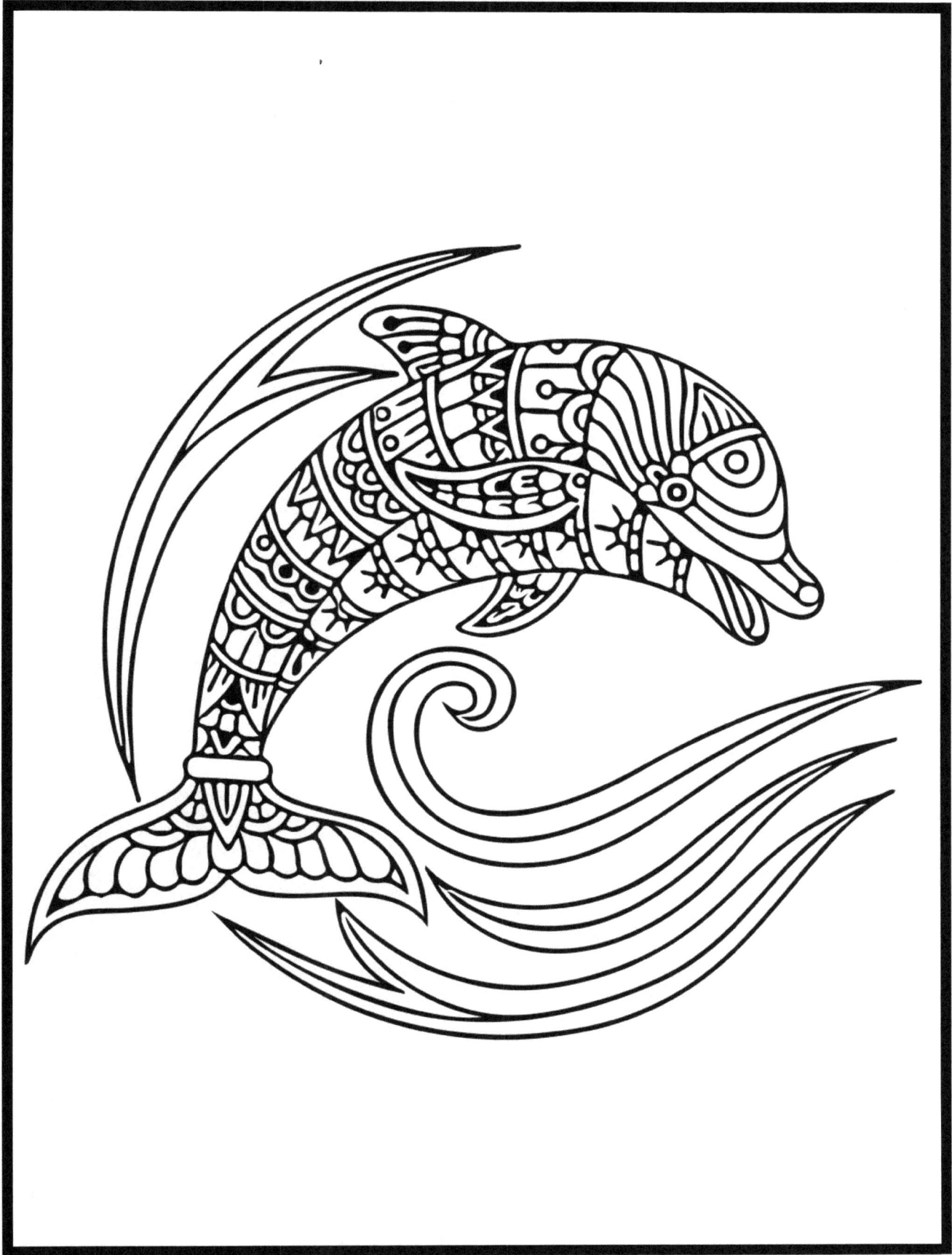

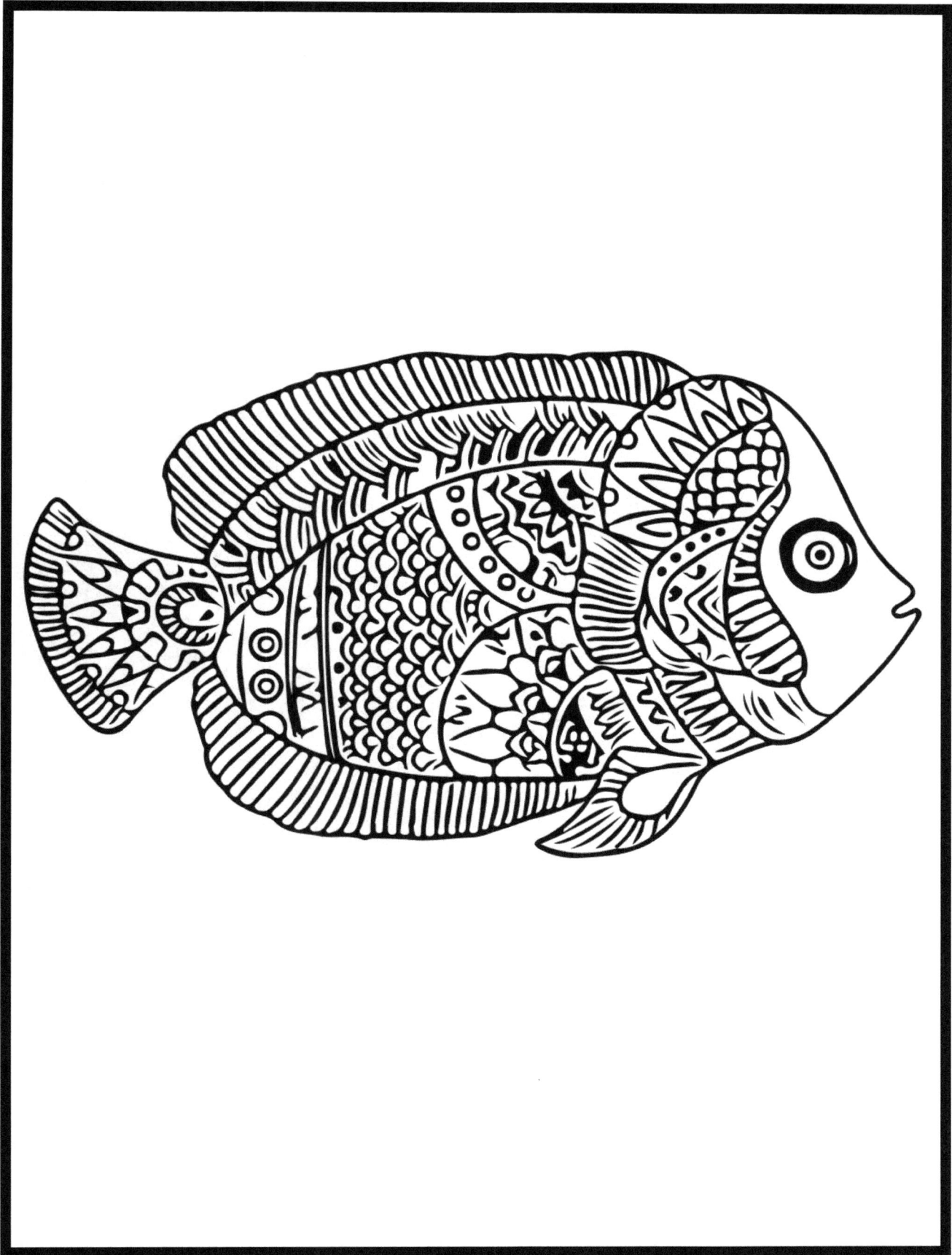

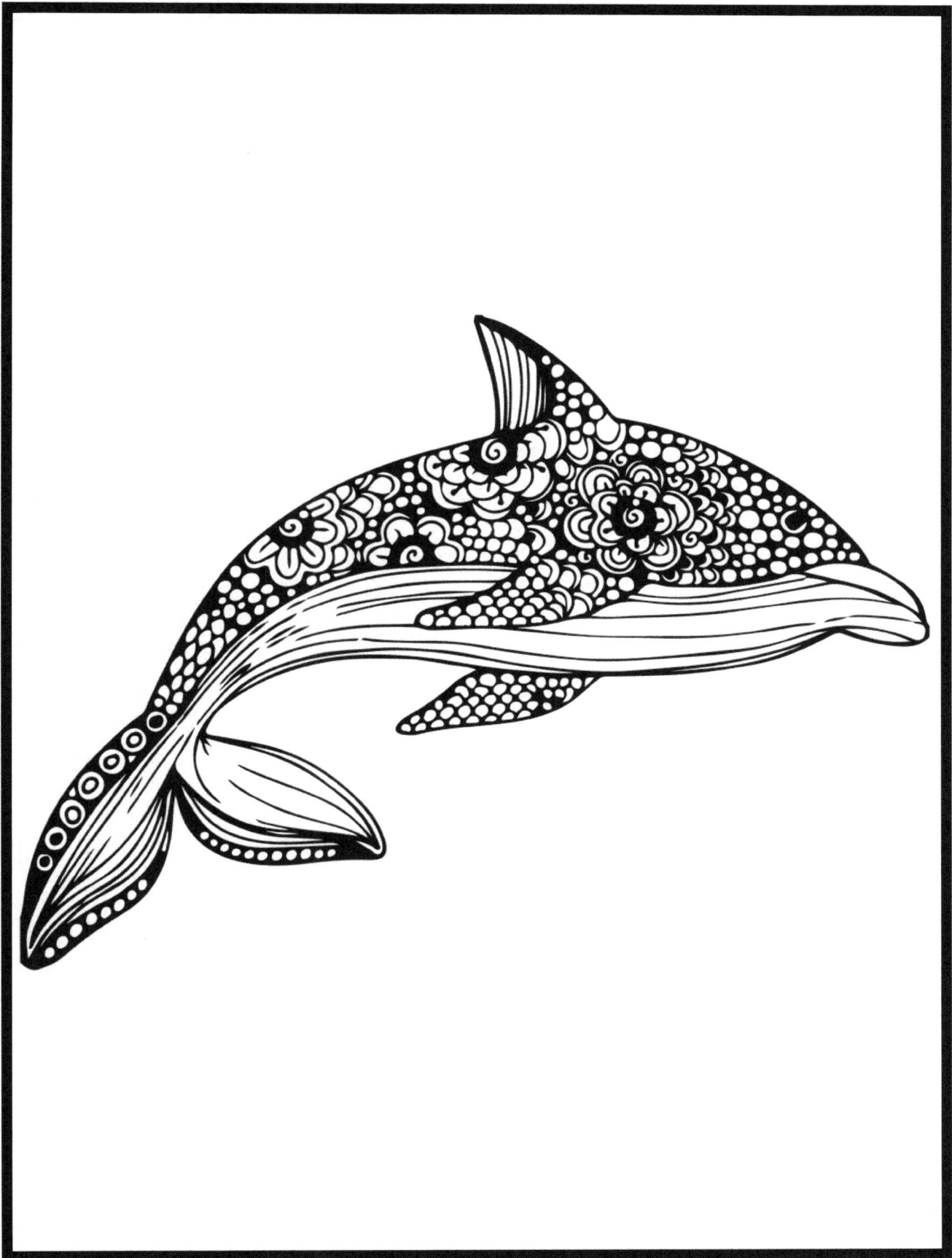

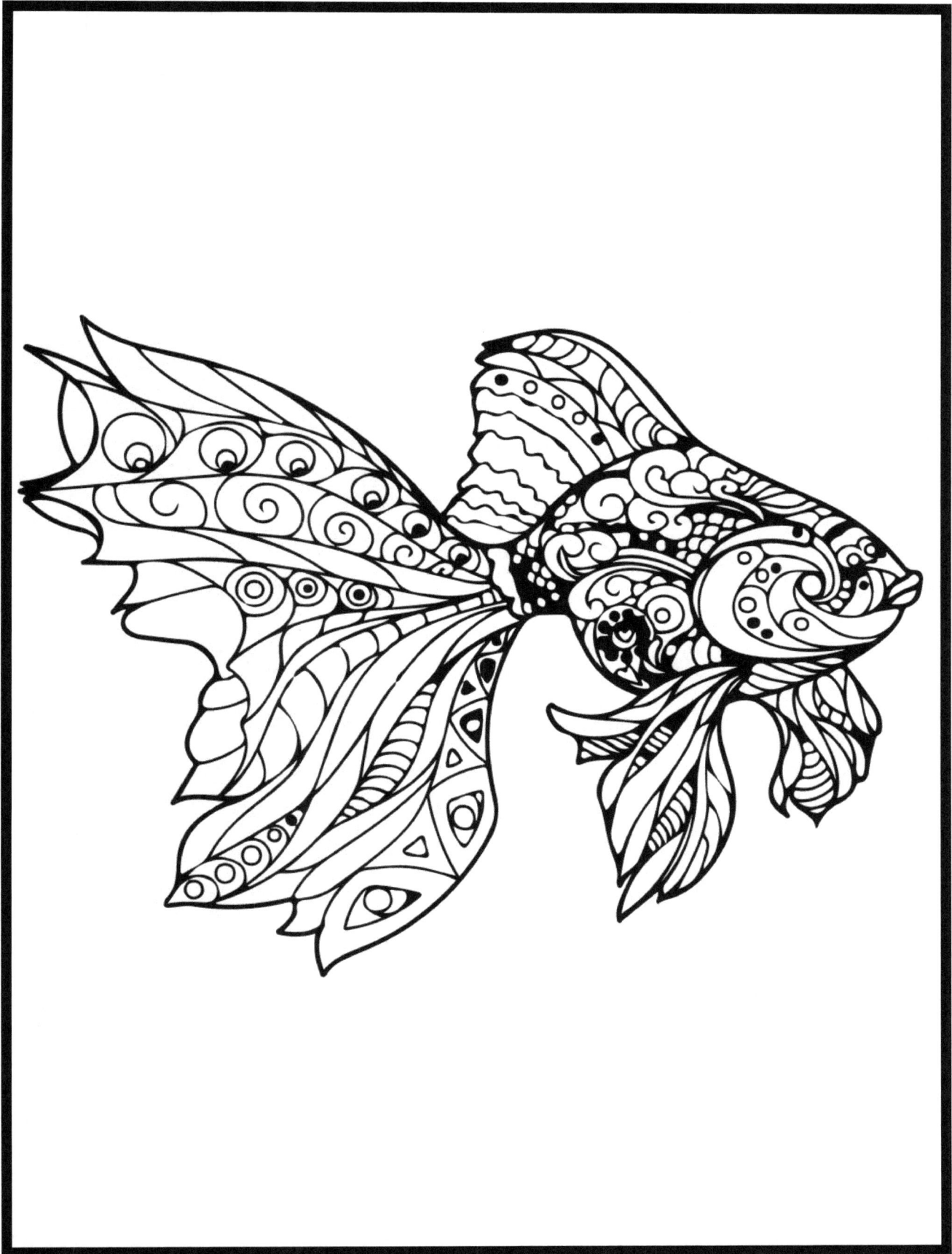

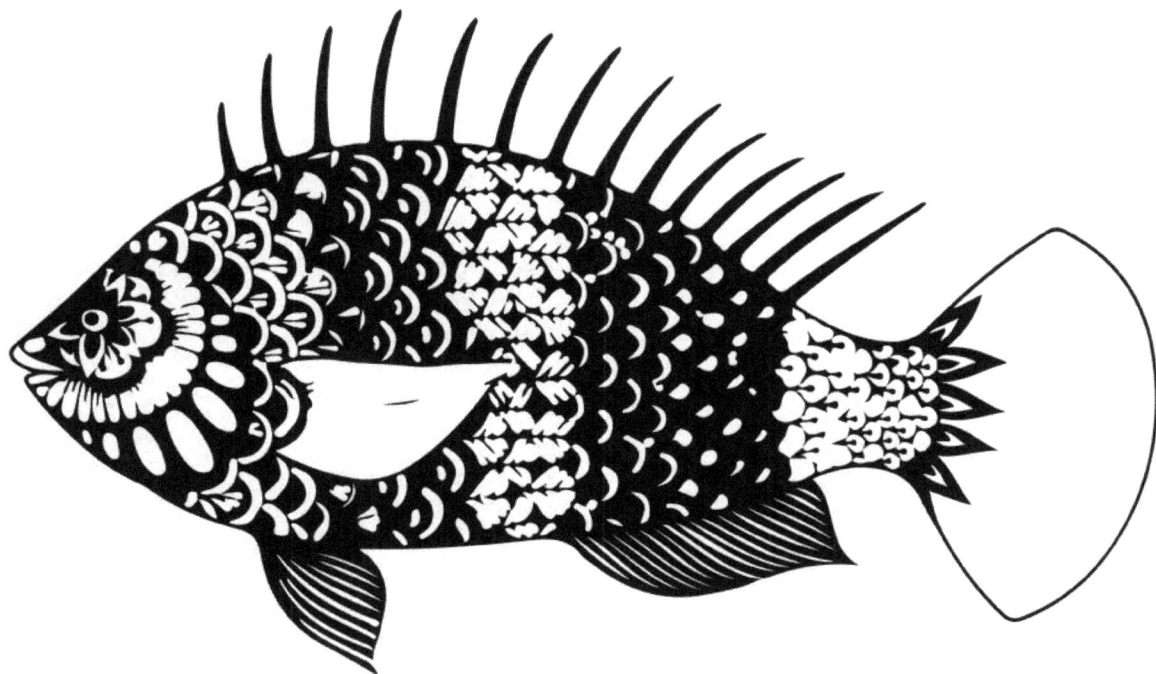

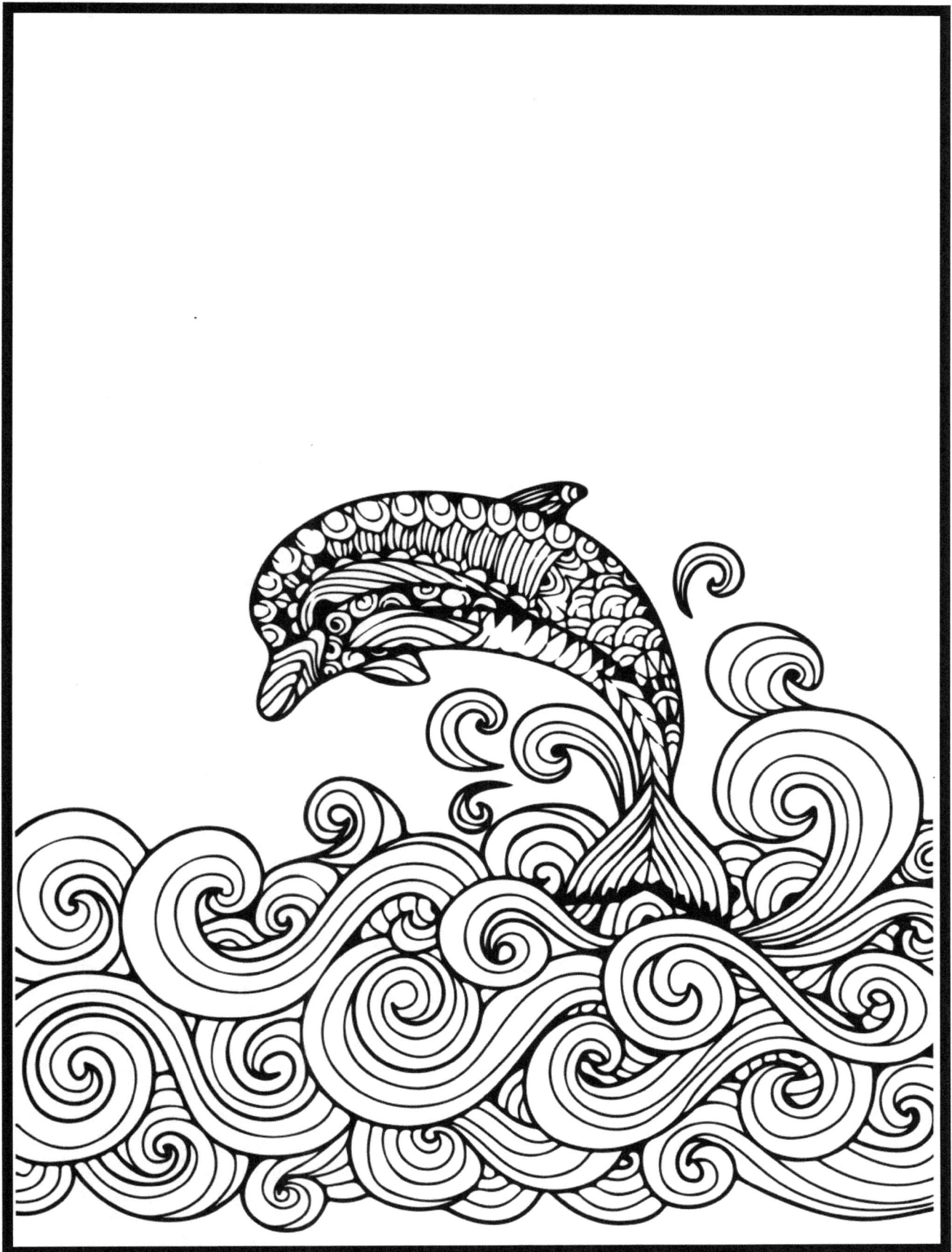

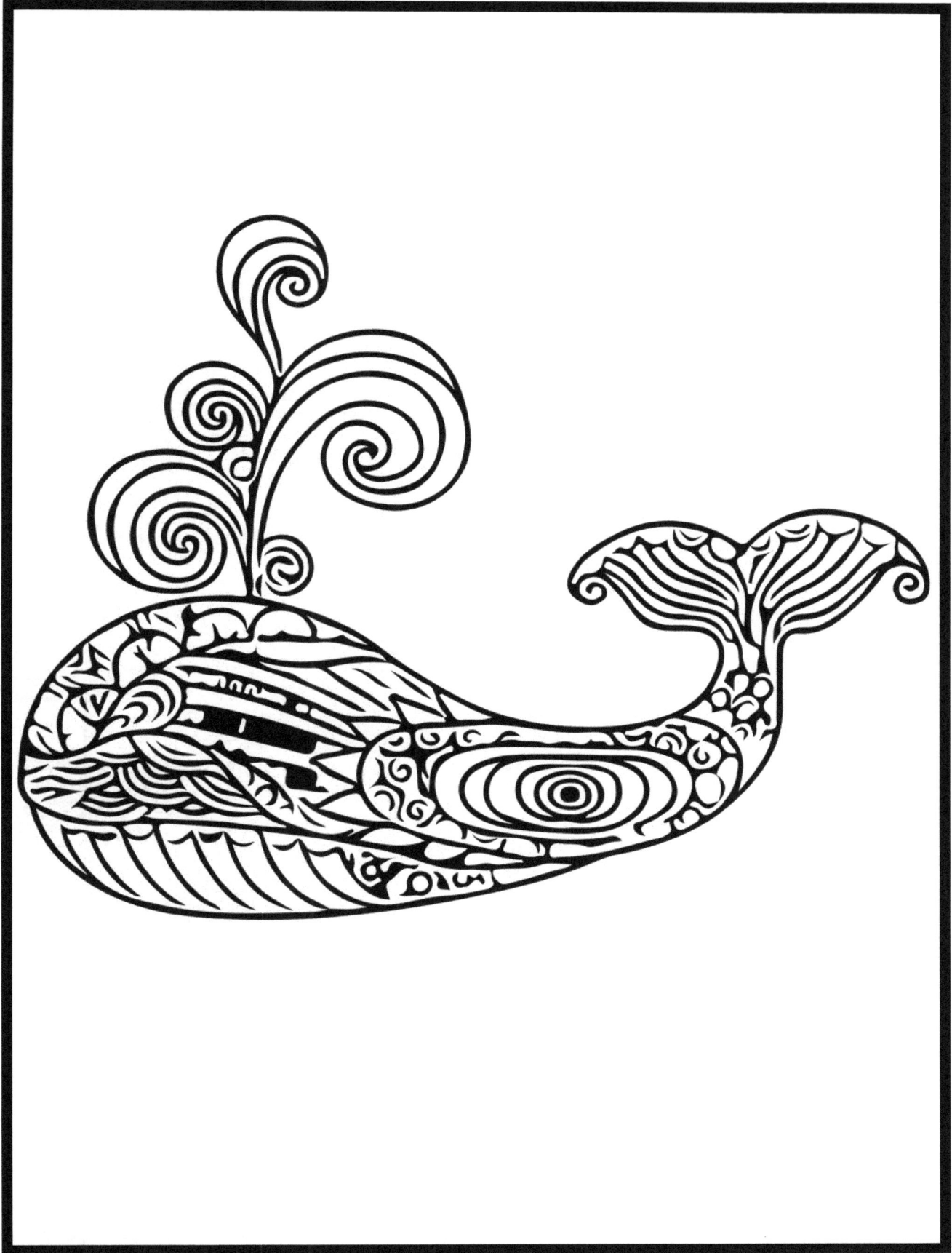

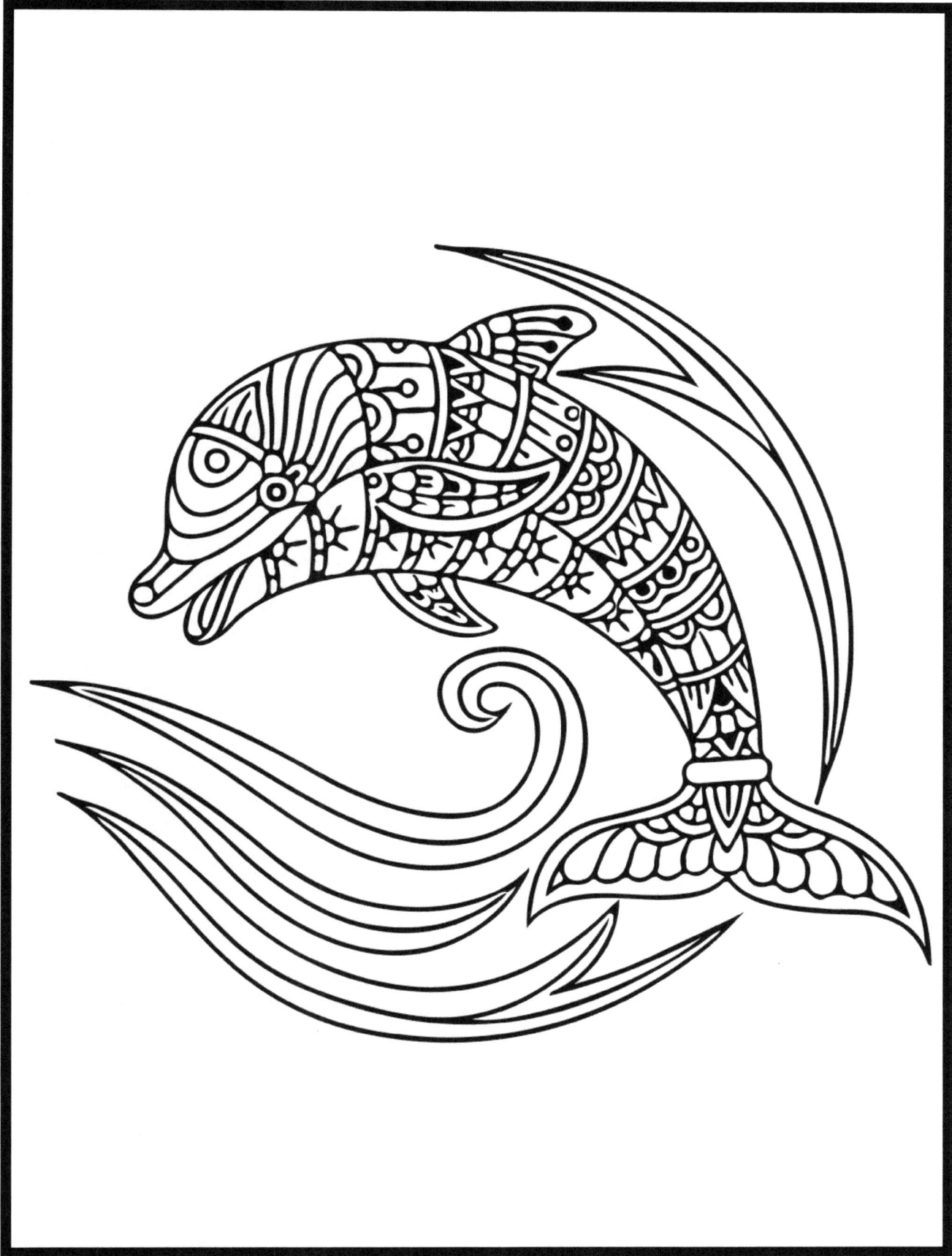

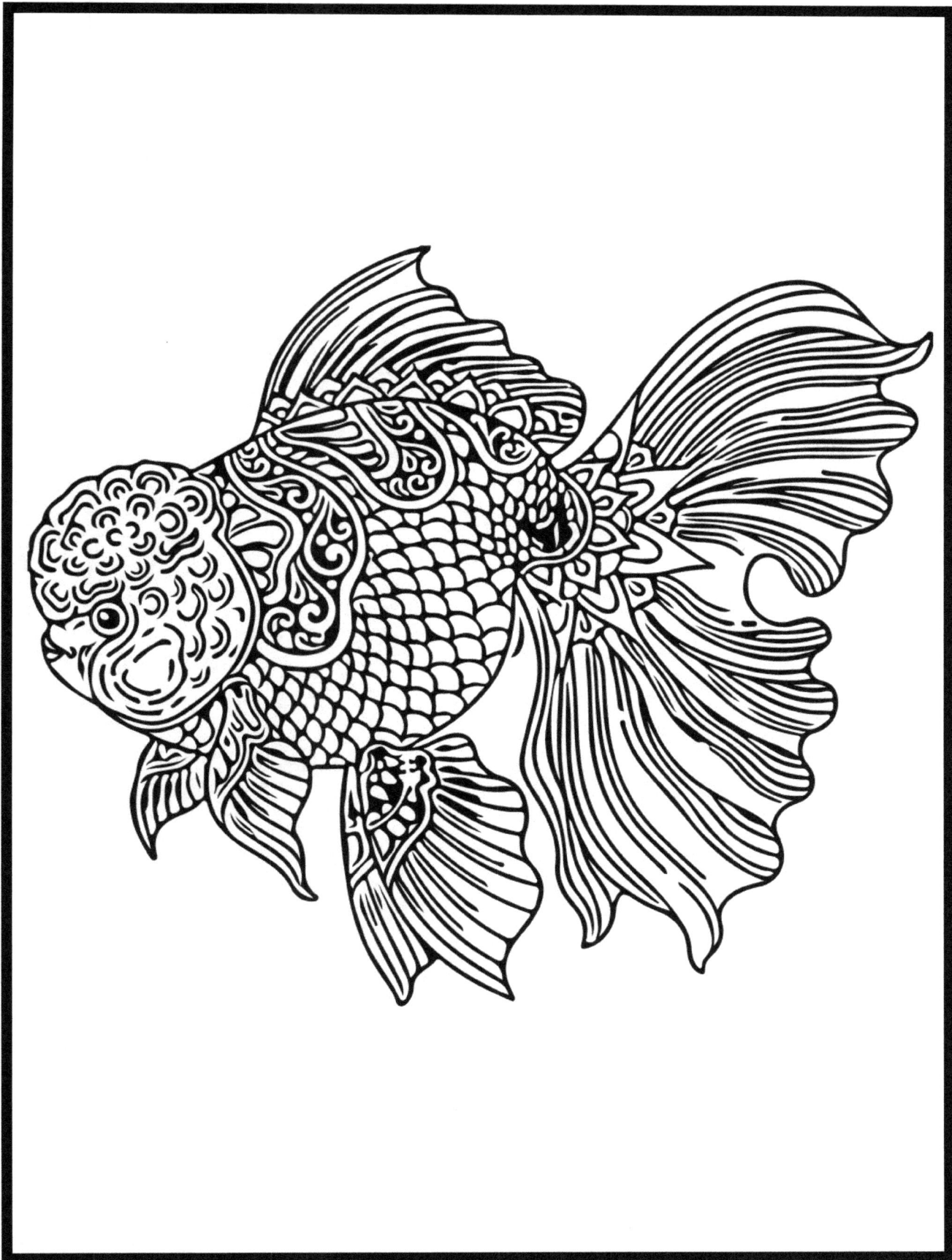

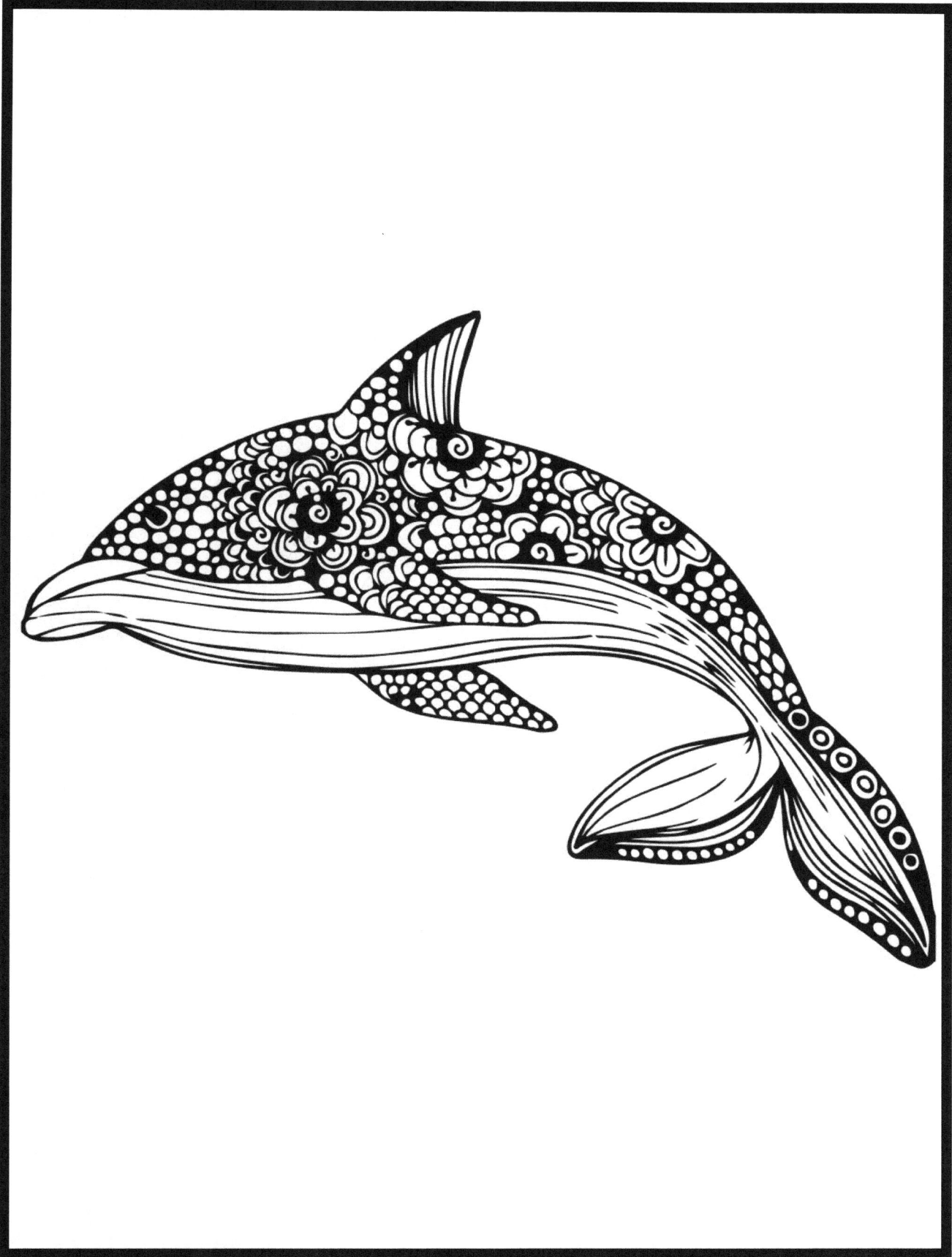

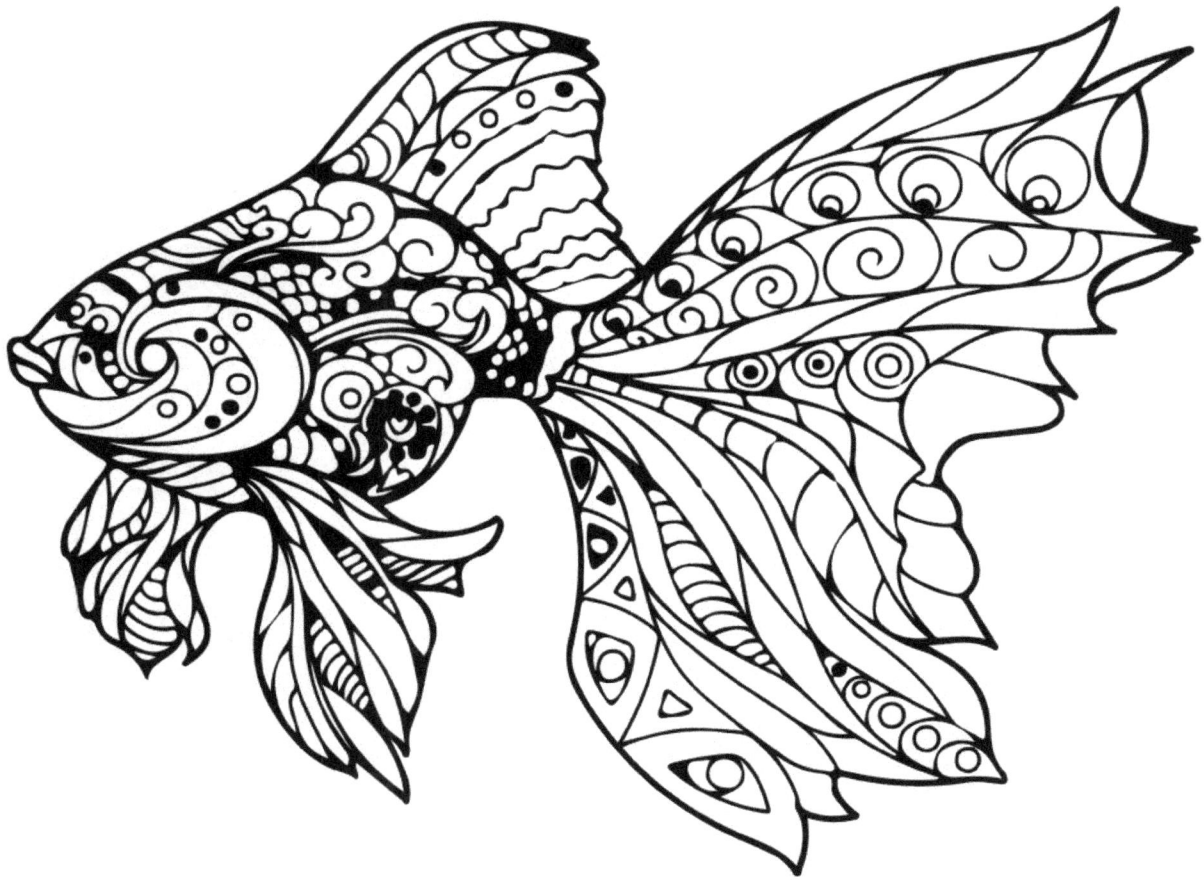

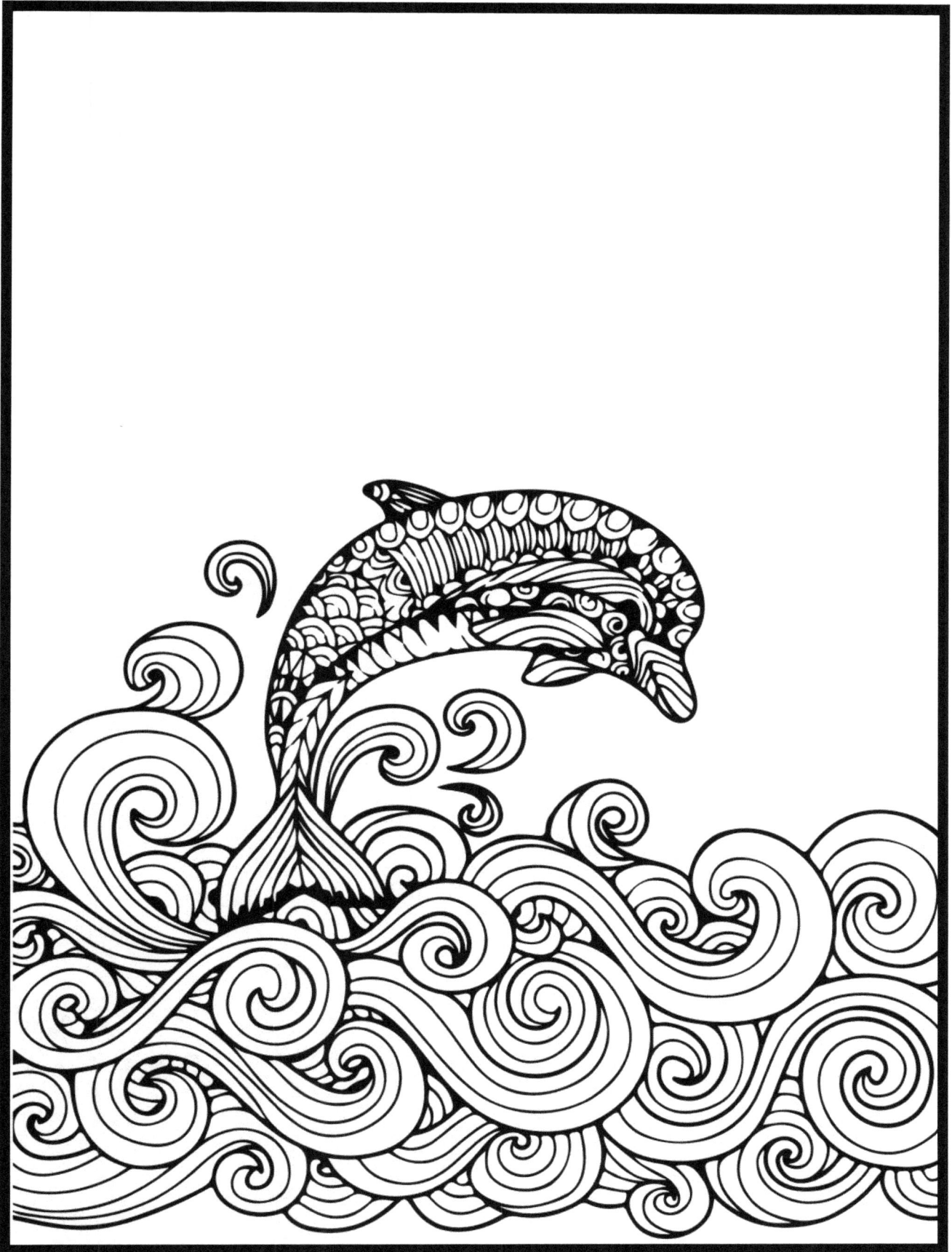

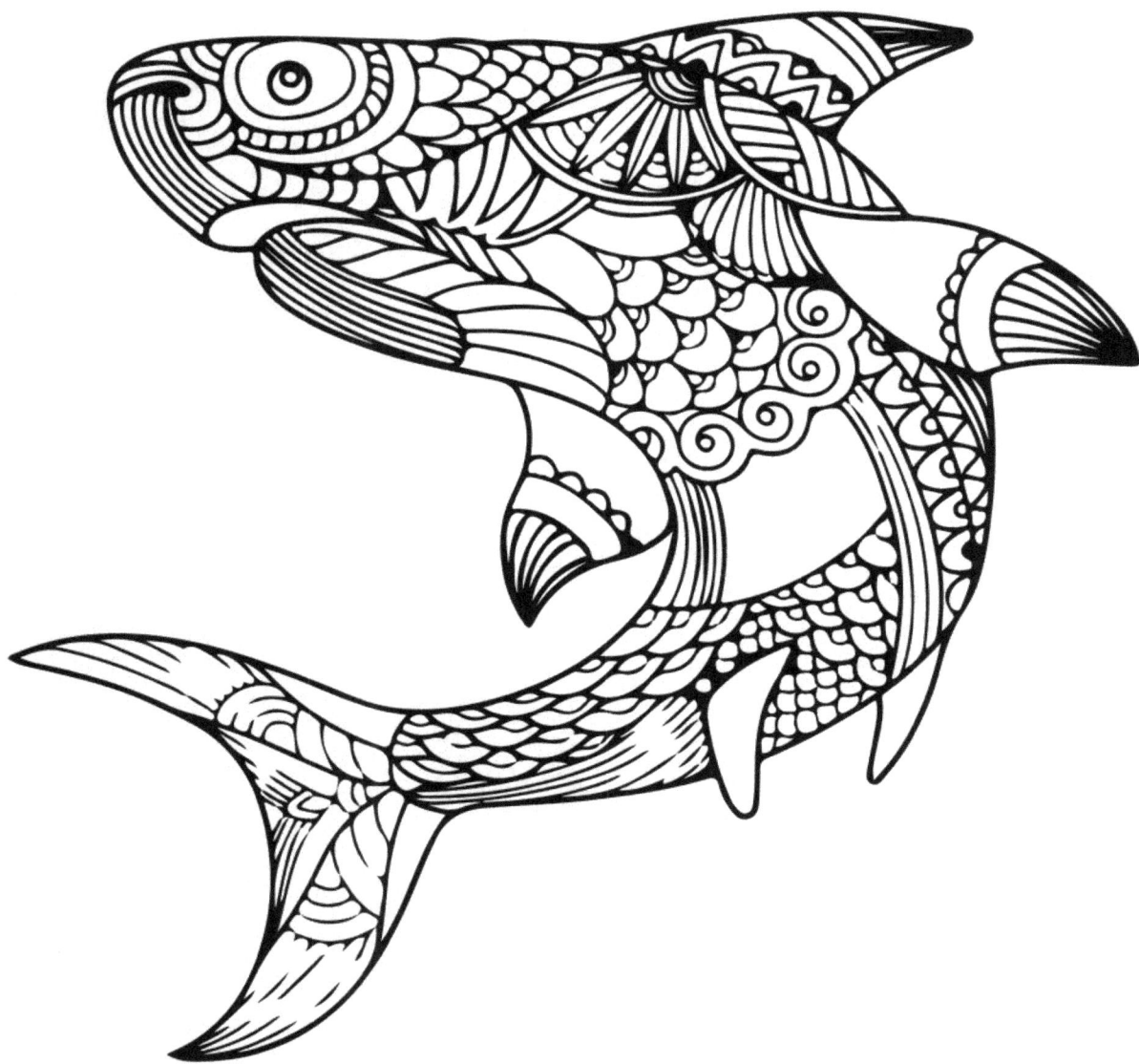

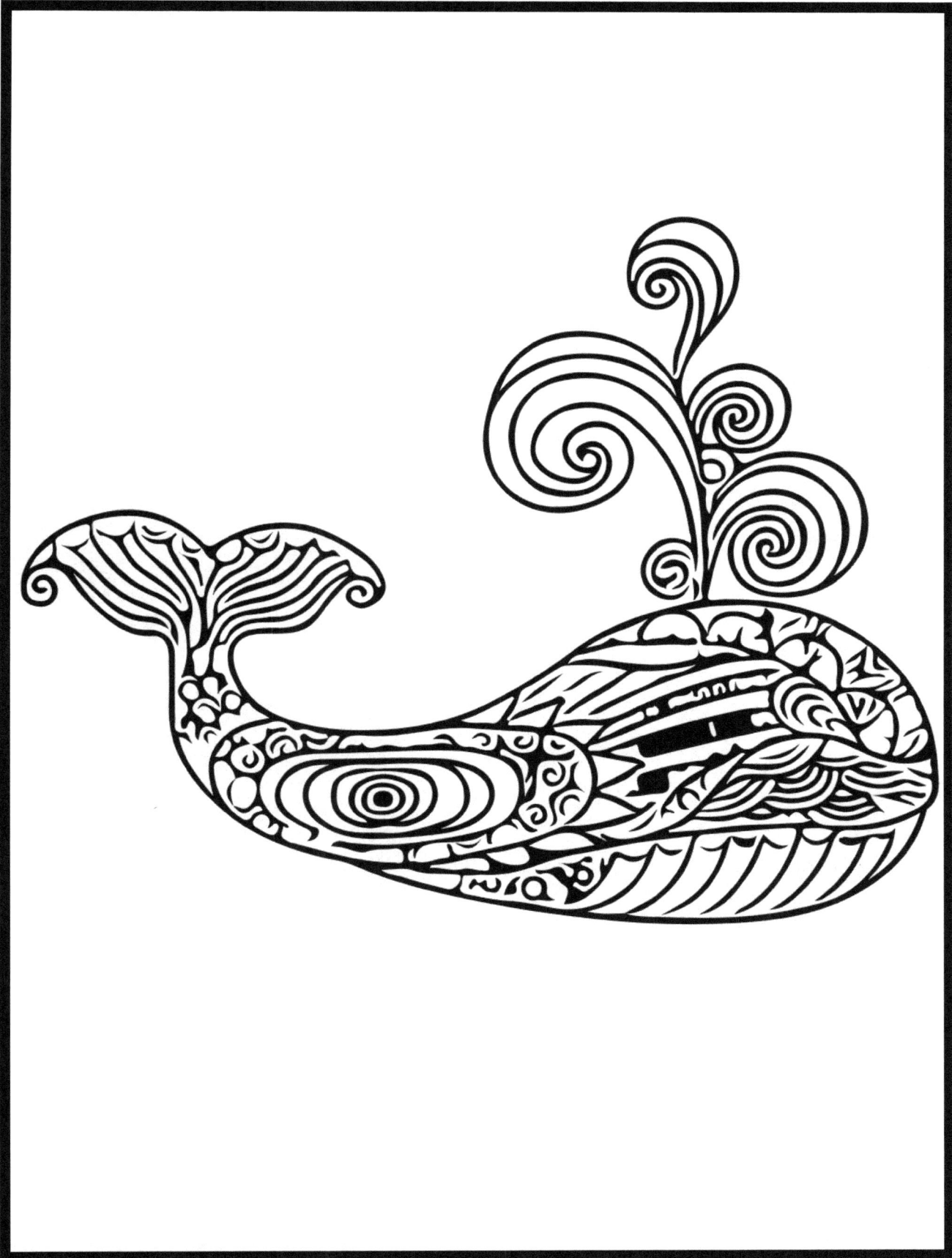

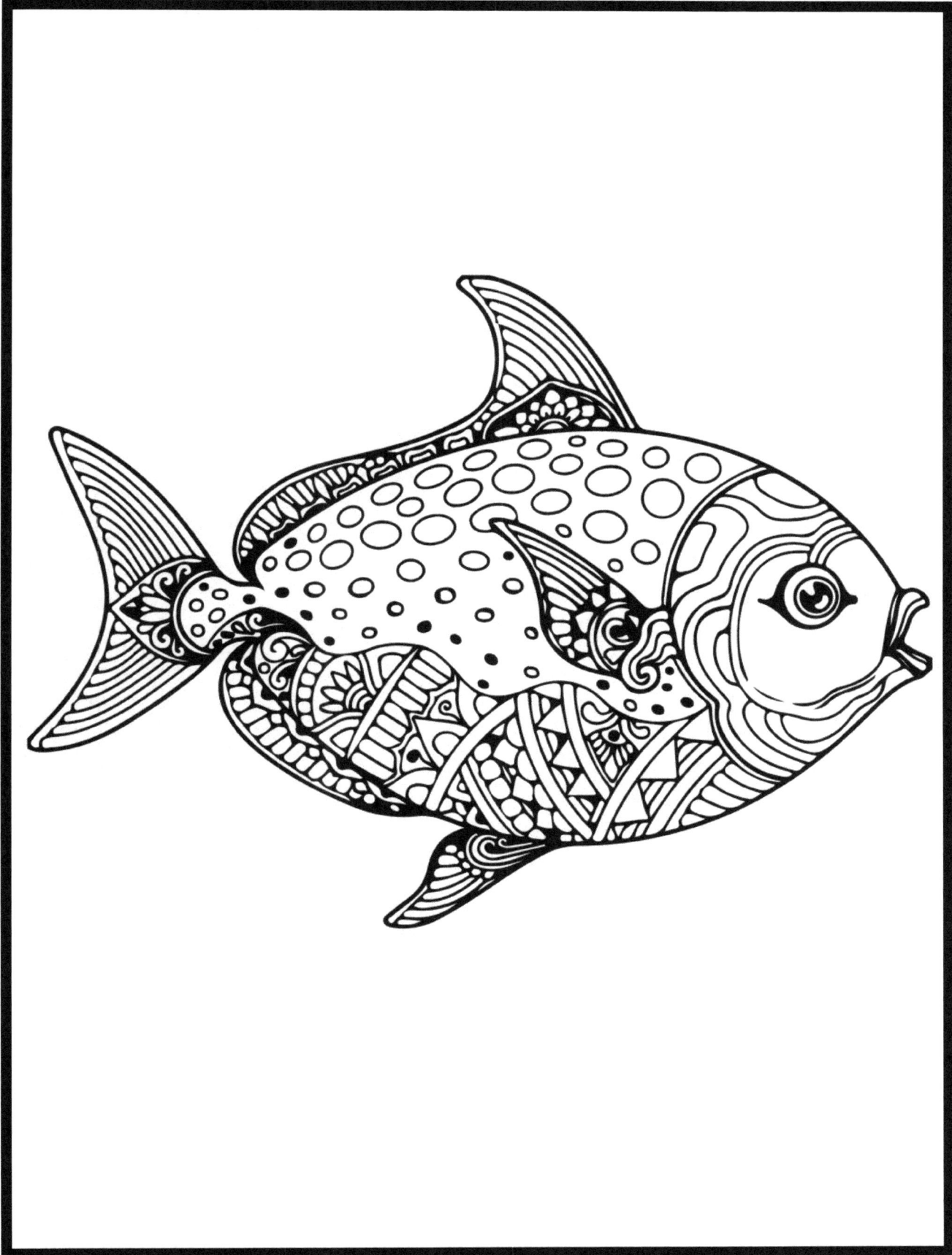

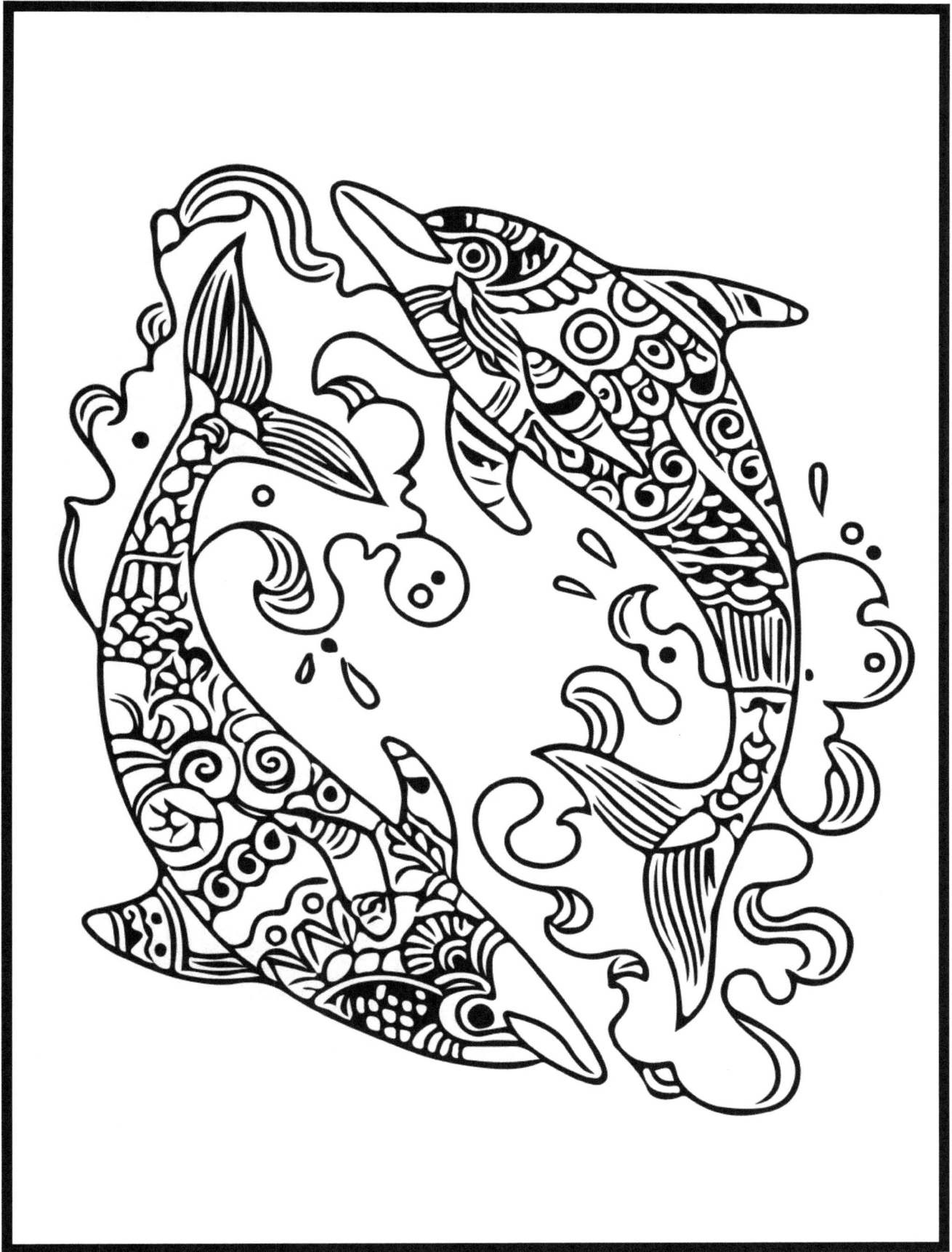

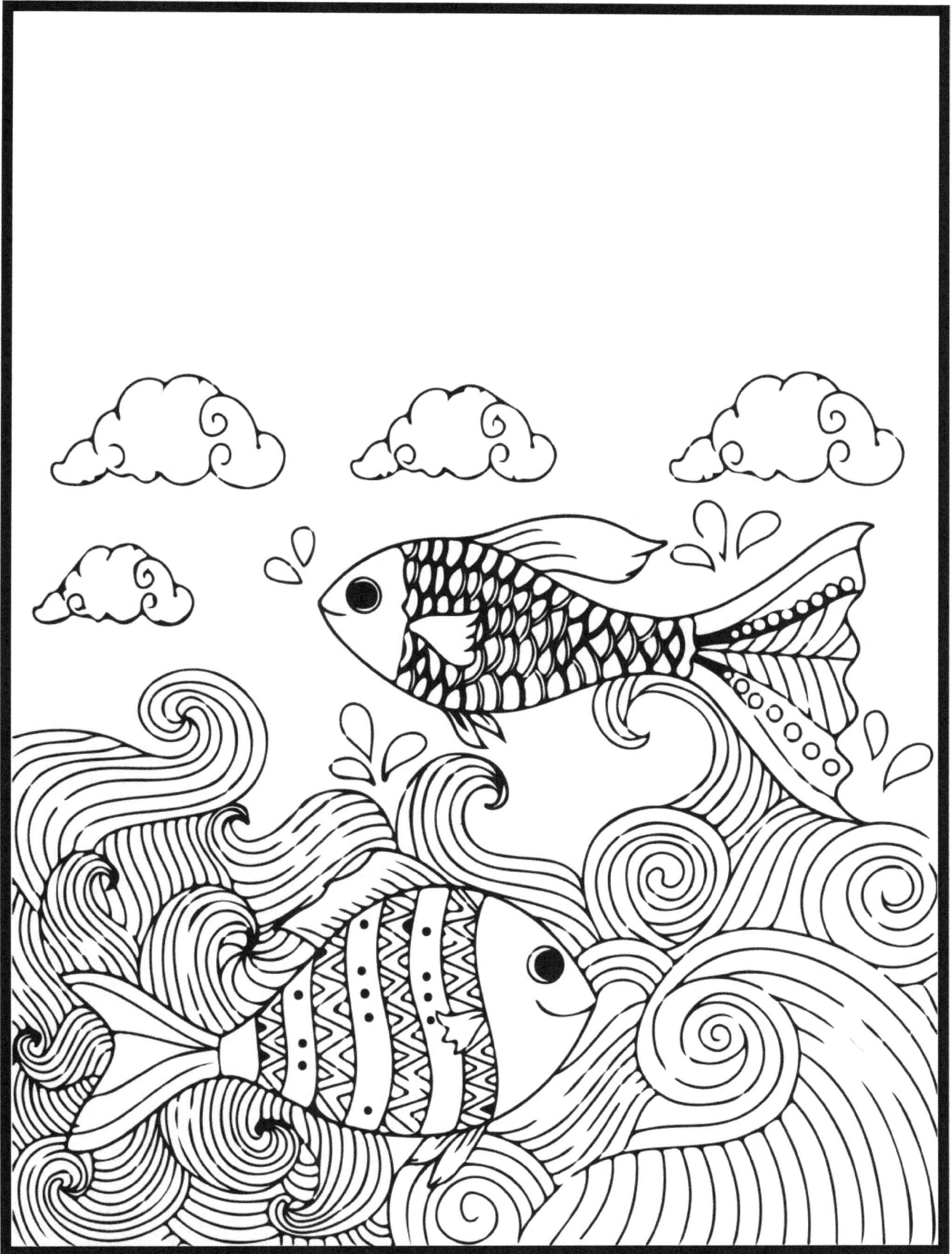

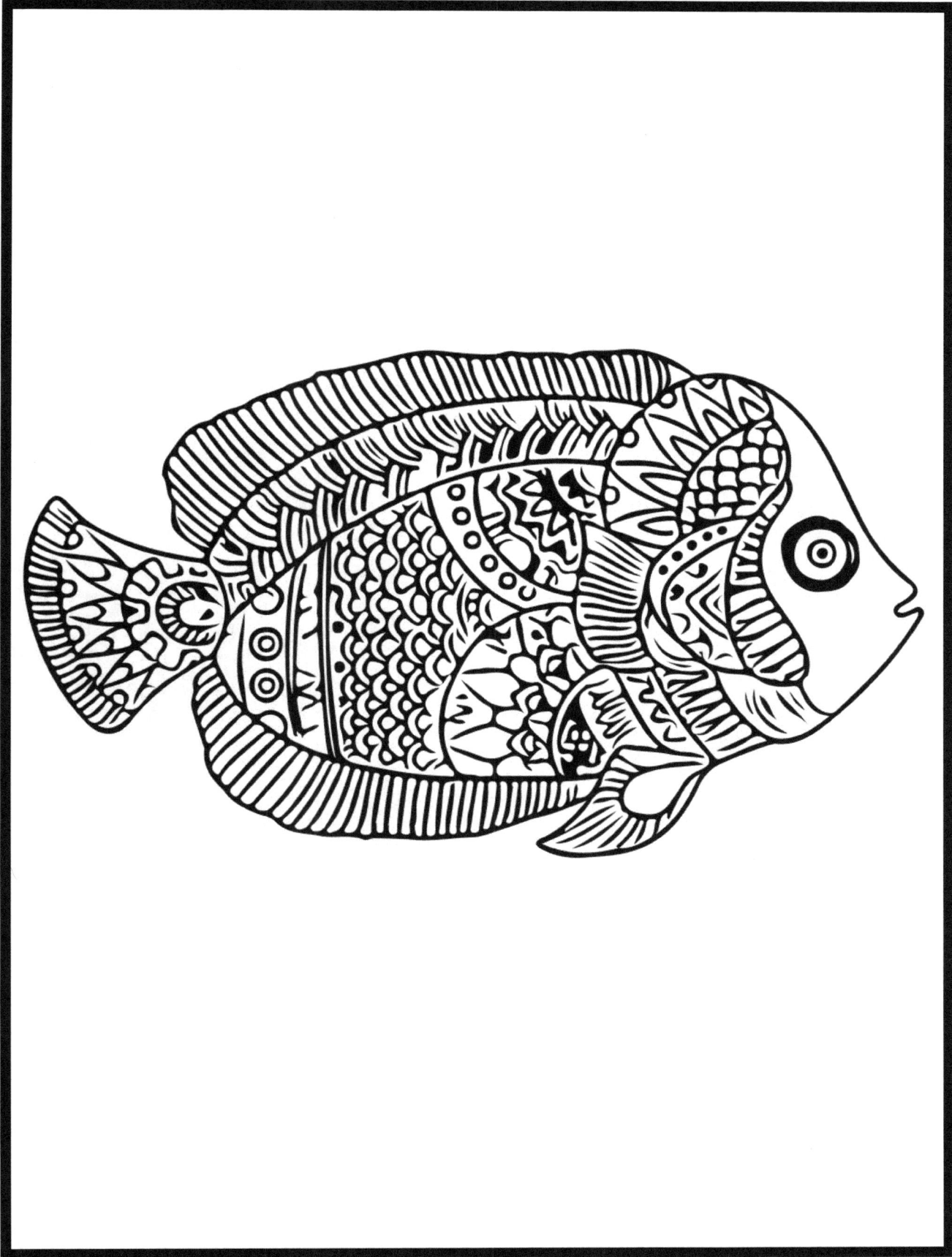

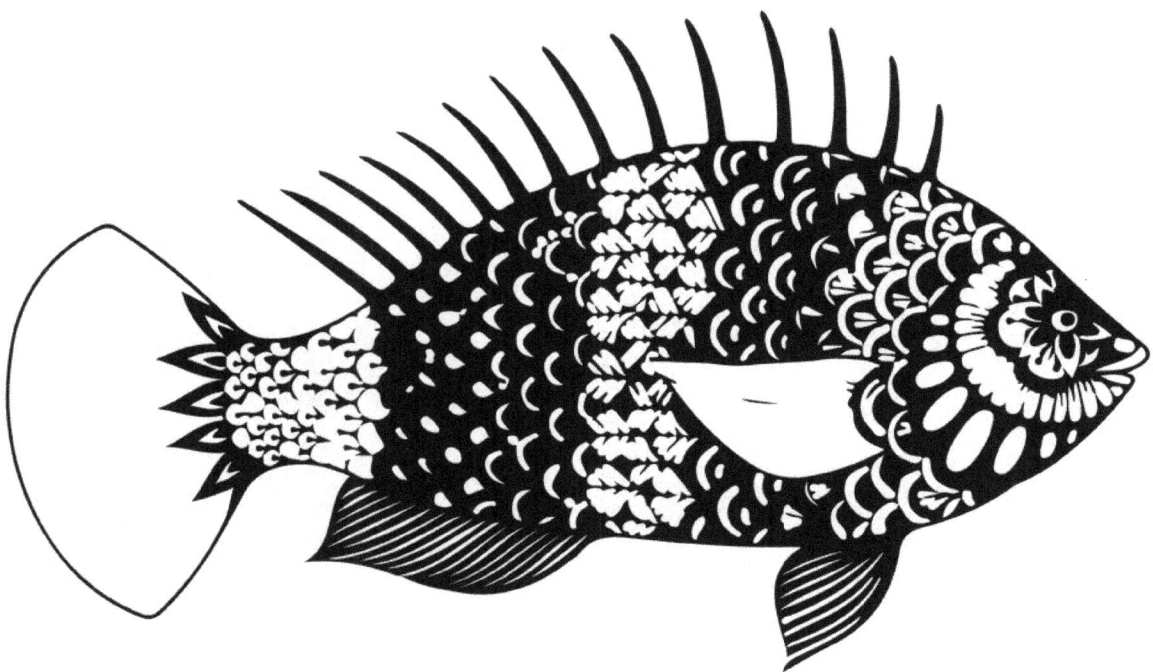

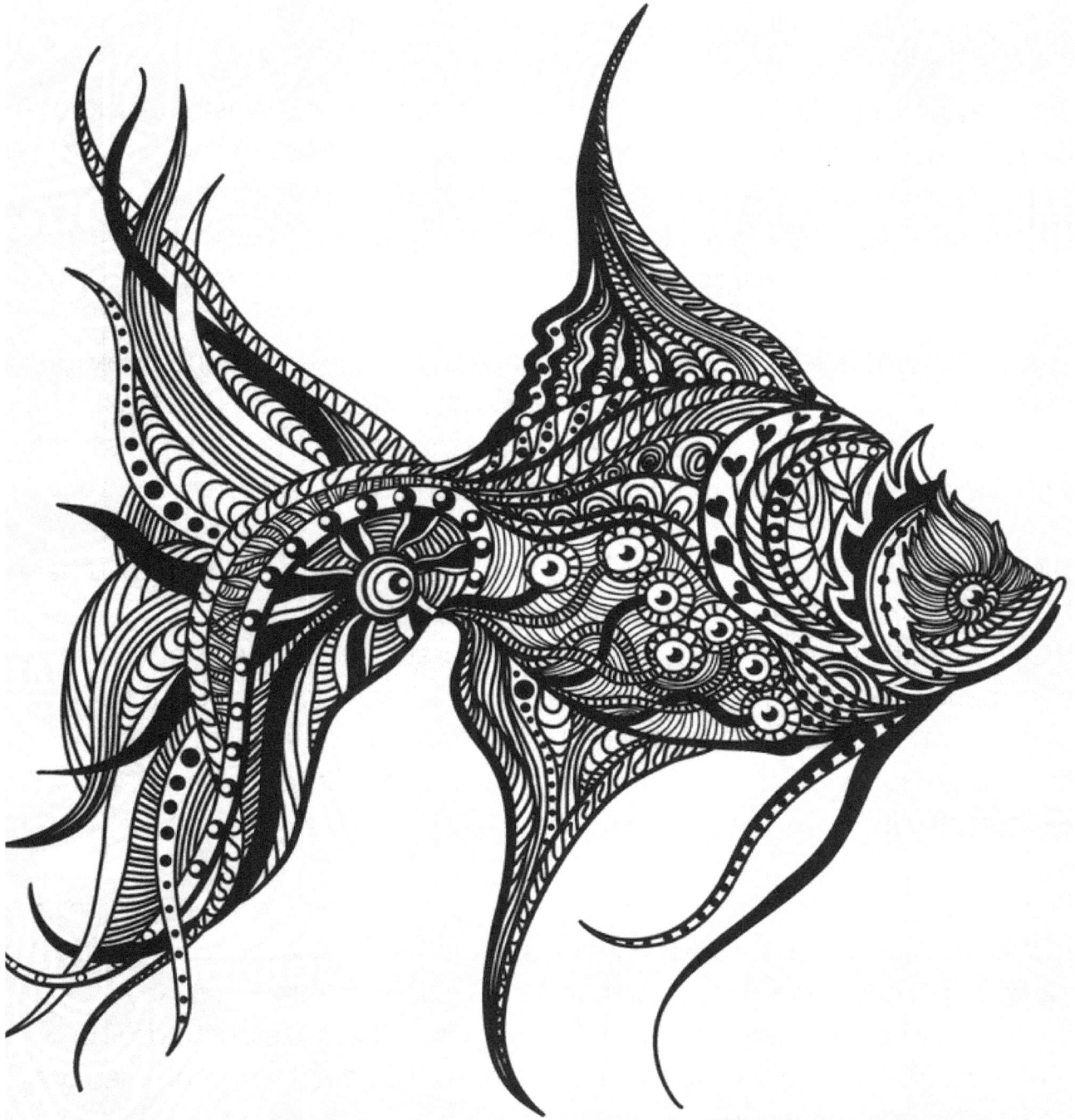

THANK YOU.

We hope that you have had many hours
of fun with our book and liked it
as much as we enjoyed working on it.

Your feedback
is very important to us.

Please let us know how you like our book at:
david.c.morgan@gmail.com

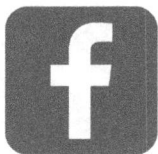

f /davidcmorgan

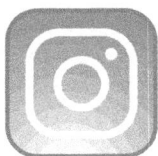

⊙ /davidcmorgan

CPSIA information can be obtained
at www.ICGtesting.com
Printed in the USA
BVHW051935250521
608097BV00003B/946